MEET THE GREATS

Mahatma GANDHI

TIM COOKE

Gareth Stevens
PUBLISHING

Please visit our website, www.garethstevens.com. For a free color catalog of all our high-quality books, call toll free 1-800-542-2595 or fax 1-877-542-2596.

Cataloging-in-Publication Data

Names: Cooke, Tim.
Title: Mahatma Gandhi / Tim Cooke.
Description: New York : Gareth Stevens Publishing, 2019. | Series: Meet the greats | Includes glossary and index.
Identifiers: LCCN ISBN 9781538225851 (pbk.) | ISBN 9781538225844 (library bound)
Subjects: LCSH: Gandhi, Mahatma, 1869-1948–Juvenile literature. | Statesmen–India–Biography–Juvenile literature. | Nationalists–India–Biography–Juvenile literature. | Lawyers–India–Biography–Juvenile literature. | India–Politics and government–1919-1947–Juvenile literature. | South Africa–Politics and government–1836-1909–Juvenile literature.
Classification: LCC DS481.G3 C66 2019 | DDC 954.03'5092 B–dc23

Published in 2019 by
Gareth Stevens Publishing
111 East 14th Street, Suite 349
New York, NY 10003

For Brown Bear Books Ltd:
Editorial Director: Lindsey Lowe
Managing Editor: Tim Cooke
Children's Publisher: Anne O'Daly
Design Manager: Keith Davis
Designer and illustrator: Supriya Sahai
Picture Manager: Sophie Mortimer

Concept development: Square and Circus / Brown Bear Books Ltd

Picture Credits: Front Cover: Character artwork, Supriya Sahai. Interior: Columbia Education: 15t; Express Newspapers: 41tt; Getty Images: Keystone, 38, Margaret Bourke White, 42; Library of Congress: 11; National Portrait Gallery: 10b; Public Domain: 13, 18, Agence de Presse Meruisse 28, Dr Graham Beards, 23, British Library, 14, 34, English Heritage, 10t, grandhiserve, 29, Heritage Images, 31b, Houston Culture, 43, Photo Division/Government of India, 35, Private Collection, 9, Rammanohar Beohar Sinha, 33, Claude TRUONG-NGOC, 25b, Irana Wao, 32, Loo Kok Wee Wilson/Flickr: Delhi, 41b, Yann, 31t, 39; Robert Hunt Library: 15b, 22, 25t; Shutterstock: Anando Art, 21t, 24, Bhumadhana Phichit, 30, PJH Pix, 20, Tantrick71, 8, 21b; Thinkstock: istockphoto 12; Topfoto: 40; Washington Post: 19.

CPSIA compliance information: Batch #CS18GS. For further information contact Gareth Stevens, New York, New York at 1-800-542-2595.

Contents

Introduction

Mahatma Gandhi guided India to freedom from British rule. His life inspired millions of people.

When Mohandas Gandhi was born in 1869, India was a British **colony**. As a young man, Gandhi trained as a lawyer. It seemed he would live an ordinary **professional** life. However, a period of time spent living in South Africa helped to make Gandhi an **activist**. He protested against **discrimination** based on race, religion, or **caste**. Gandhi's followers called him "mahatma," meaning "great soul."

Back in India, Gandhi became a leader of the campaign for independence from British rule. He rejected violent protest in favor of nonviolent resistance called *satyagraha*, or "holding on to truth." *Satyagraha* included methods such as **fasting** and holding protest marches. Gandhi helped India gain its **independence** in August 1947. The following year he was killed by a Hindu who objected to Gandhi's attempts to accept India's Muslims into the new country.

Becoming an ACTIVIST

Gandhi was a shy boy who overcame his nervousness to become a champion of poor and disadvantaged people.

Mohandas Karamchand Gandhi was born on October 2, 1869. His family was from Porbandar, a coastal town in Gujarat State in western India. Gandhi's father, Karamchand, was the town's *dewan*, or chief minister. Gandhi's mother, Putlibai, stayed at home to raise him and his two older brothers and sister, as well as two half-sisters from his father's previous marriages. The family was wealthy enough to have servants. The Gandhis were Hindus. Putlibai prayed many times a day, and the whole family were strict vegetarians. When Mohandas was seven, the family moved inland to Rajkot.

QUICK FACTS

- Gandhi was a shy young man.
- His parents arranged for him to get married at the age of just 13. His bride, Kasturba, was also 13.

POOR STUDENT

Gandhi grew up to become one of the most influential men in the world, but he was not a very good student. He worked hard, but only got average grades. Gandhi was also very shy. He used to run home from school to avoid having to speak to anyone.

A memorial complex for Gandhi in Porbandar.

When Gandhi was 13, his parents arranged for him to marry Kasturba, the daughter of a family friend. Getting married so young was normal in India at the time. It was also common for parents to choose a partner for their child—and still is. The wedding interrupted Gandhi's studies and he missed school for a year. Gandhi and Kasturba were married for more than 62 years. When he was older, Gandhi spoke out against child marriages.

FINISHING SCHOOL

Back at school, Gandhi worked hard to please his teachers. At home, he took care of his father, who was now old and sick. His father died when Gandhi was 16. More sadness followed. Gandhi and Kasturba had a child who died soon after birth.

Gandhi graduated from high school in 1887 and went to college, but he dropped out after just one semester. A friend suggested that Gandhi should go to England to study law, so he could become a dewan like his father. Despite his shyness, Gandhi agreed. He would leave behind his young wife and their new baby son, Harilal, as well as his widowed mother, and travel to London.

Gandhi and Kasturba were married in 1882.

A NEW START

Gandhi traveled to Bombay to board a ship to England. Before he left, the leaders of his **merchant** caste, the Bania, warned him not to travel overseas. They believed that travelers in the West became corrupted by eating meat and drinking alcohol. Although Gandhi vowed to stick to the principles of his Hindu religion, the elders declared that, if he went, they would declare him an **outcast**. He would become one of the Dalit, or Untouchables—the lowest caste, who were shunned by other Indians. Bravely, Gandhi ignored his elders. He set sail for England on September 4, 1888.

A plaque marks Gandhi's rooms in London.

The Dalit face violence, discrimination, and poverty.

In the late 1800s, London was a crowded, busy city.

LONDON LIFE

Gandhi found London very different from India. He tried to behave as an English gentleman did, and even bought himself a top hat. One problem was the food. Gandhi found it hard to find dishes without meat until, on one of his long walks around London, he found a vegetarian restaurant. He finally had not just somewhere to eat but somewhere to meet other vegetarians.

Gandhi studied hard and passed his law exams at University College, London, on June 10, 1891. To celebrate, the London Vegetarian Society held a dinner in his honor—but he was too shy to give the speech he had prepared!

BACK TO INDIA

After three years in London, Gandhi returned home. His brother, Laxmidas, met him with the sad news that their mother had died while Gandhi had been away. The homecoming was made worse when the Bania caste followed through with their threat. They only accepted Gandhi back into the caste after he bathed in a sacred river.

Gandhi had studied to be a **barrister**. The job involved standing up in a law court in order to defend his clients. Gandhi soon discovered that his shyness meant that he hated appearing in court! He quit his job in Bombay and moved back to Rajkot, where he took a desk job in a law firm.

Gandhi did not enjoy speaking in court.

Gandhi only intended to stay in South Africa for a year.

ANOTHER MOVE

Gandhi heard that a Porbandar merchant in South Africa needed a lawyer. He took the job and moved to South Africa in April 1893. Kasturba had just had another son, so she stayed in India.

In South Africa, Gandhi was thrown off a train when a white man complained about an Indian being in a first-class carriage. Gandhi had a first-class ticket. In Pretoria, Gandhi was again treated badly because of his race. He decided the time had come to act. He asked the Indians in Pretoria to a meeting and made his first public speech. He said it was time to stand up for the rights of Indians in South Africa—and that he would lead the fight.

The British IN INDIA

Europeans began setting up trading posts in India in the 1600s. By the 1800s, the British East India Company had defeated its rivals and taken control of all of India.

Although the company was a private business, it ran India like a government, with its own governors and armed forces. In 1857, Indian soldiers working for the British company revolted against changes in military regulations. The unrest against the British soon spread to civilians. The British used regular soldiers to defeat the Indian **Mutiny**.

In 1858, the British parliament passed the Government of India Act. The act transferred control of India from the East India Company to the British government and Queen Victoria. This created what became known as the British Raj, or "rule."

British officials visit a ruler of one of India's many states.

Many of the senior government posts were filled by British army officers.

The British government sent officials to govern India. They were headed by the Queen's representative, the viceroy. These British officials controlled all aspects of Indian life. They ran India for the benefit of the British economy rather than to improve the lives of Indians.

British laws increasingly discriminated against local people. They made English the national language, and created an education system based on British schools. They built railroads to connect economically important cities in the huge country. But the British in India never numbered more than 100,000, at a time when the Indian population was 380 million.

Englishwomen pulled in rickshaws during the Raj.

Mobilizing Against THE BRITISH

Gandhi lived in South Africa for 21 years. When he finally returned home to India, he was greeted as a hero.

Like India, South Africa was part of the vast British Empire. Indians living in South Africa had few rights. They were not allowed outdoors after 9:00 p.m., they could not walk on public footpaths, and they were forced to pay extra taxes. Their marriages were not legal because South African law only recognized Christian marriages and almost all Indians in South Africa were Muslims or Hindus. They could not vote. Gandhi decided to stay on in South Africa to try to improve the rights of his fellow Indians. After three years, he brought his family from India to live with him.

QUICK FACTS

- Gandhi's campaigns against discrimination in South Africa made him famous.
- He followed a policy of nonviolent protest.

A PERIOD OF ACTIVISM

In 1899, the Boer War (1899–1902) broke out between the British and the Boers, who were descendants of Dutch settlers in South Africa. Gandhi **mobilized** 1,000 Indian volunteers to collect wounded British soldiers from the battlefield and nurse them. He hoped this show of **loyalty** would improve the treatment of Indians in South Africa. He was wrong. Gandhi thought carefully about his next step. He decided to begin a series of nonviolent protests, and developed his philosophy of *satyagraha*. This was soon put to the test.

Gandhi (middle row, center) formed a medical corps in the Boer War.

In 1906, the South African government passed the "Black Act." The act stated that all Indian males should be fingerprinted and carry identification passes at all times. No other group of people had to do this. Gandhi urged his followers to resist the act by refusing to register. As a result, he and many other Indians were sent to jail.

Gandhi (center) and the staff of his law office in South Africa.

SUCCESSFUL STRIKE

In 1913, Gandhi organized a **strike** of Indian coal miners to protest an unfair tax the South African government imposed on them. Supported by local Indian businessmen, who gave them food and money, the miners went on strike until the government backed down. In July 1914, the South African government passed the Indian Relief Act, which ended the unfair taxes and recognized marriages of all faiths. Gandhi's tactic of nonviolence had worked! Following the strike, Gandhi felt that his work in South Africa was done. It was time to go home to India.

Gandhi lived near the city of Ahmadabad in Gujurat.

A FREE INDIA?

Gandhi returned to India with a goal in mind. He wanted the British to give India independence. He believed that Indians would be able to show the British that they were more than capable of ruling themselves. He also wanted to change some of India's social traditions, such as the caste system and the treatment of the Untouchables.

A NEW ASHRAM

In South Africa, Gandhi had founded settlements where people could follow the *satyagraha* by living simply as a community, or **ashram**. In India, he created an ashram near the city of Ahmadabad, the center of India's textile industry. In the ashram, people spun yarn, grew their own food, prayed, and studied.

A simple spinning wheel that Gandhi used to spin cotton.

Gandhi spent an hour every day spinning yarn. He did this to show Indians that they could be self-sufficient. The British Empire earned a lot of income from cotton. The cotton was grown in India but made into cloth in England before being sold in India. By making their own cloth, Gandhi believed Indians would take profit from the British.

This is Gandhi's house in Sabarmati Ashram.

WORLD WAR I

Indian troops wear gas masks during a drill in France in World War I.

When Britain joined World War I (1914–1918) in Europe, its whole empire entered the conflict, including India. Many Indians volunteered to join the British Army. Although Gandhi believed in nonviolence, he hoped that India's loyalty might persuade the British to grant independence. Once again, he was wrong. In 1919, the British made it illegal to protest against their government in India. Gandhi called on Indians to challenge the new law peacefully. A series of strikes paralyzed India on April 6, 1919. There were a few outbreaks of violence, and the British feared an uprising.

KILLING AT AMRITSAR

On April 12, British General Reginald Dyer banned meetings in the northern city of Amritsar. The following day was a holiday. Up to 10,000 people gathered in a square to celebrate. Dyer ordered his men to open fire on the peaceful gathering. More than 400 people died and many were wounded. As news of the **massacre** spread, there was outrage. It was time to fight back.

THE FIGHT BACK BEGINS

Gandhi's response to the massacre was to refuse to cooperate with the British in India. He asked people not to buy British goods and to stop working for the British government in India. He also decided to reinforce the fact that he was an Indian. In 1921, Gandhi started to wear the *dhoti*, the white cotton **loincloth** worn by ordinary Indian men. He wore the garment for the rest of his life.

To make sure as many Indians as possible heard his message of nonviolence in the drive for independence, Gandhi traveled around India to speak, visiting small villages. He also began fasting.

Bullet holes are still visible in the walls at the scene of the massacre of Amritsar.

Gandhi's PHILOSOPHY

Gandhi used a whole new form of protest against the British in India. He called it *satyagraha*, from the Hindu words *satya* "truth" and *agraha* "force."

Gandhi did not believe violence was ever justified. However, he rejected the idea of passive resistance, or refusing to obey British laws. Instead, he wanted to show that "truth," or behaving in a morally justified way, had the power to overcome laws that were unjust.

A statue of Gandhi in the Sabarmati Ashram.

There were three parts to *satyagraha*: nonviolence, noncooperation, and nonpossession. The first two meant using only nonviolent ways to break the law, such as by striking. Nonpossession meant only owning a few personal possessions.

Martin Luther King adopted nonviolent protest to improve rights for African–Americans in the 1960s.

Gandhi practiced what he preached. He owned little, and shared what he had. He believed that *satyagraha* was a final option for protest when it was clear that all other attempts to solve a problem had failed. Gandhi insisted that *satyagraha* should always follow a strict code. It had to have a clear goal, and protestors should always be willing to stop and talk if their opponents started to listen to their arguments. Protestors should also accept the consequences of their actions, even if that meant imprisonment. Gandhi went to jail many times for breaking the law.

Aung San Suu Kyi spent 15 years under house arrest.

Gandhi's ideas spread beyond India. Martin Luther King Jr. adopted the philosophy of nonviolence when he led the civil rights movement in the 1960s. Aung San Suu Kyi later used similar methods to protest against military government in Burma.

Heading for INDEPENDENCE

Gandhi was popular across India. However, the British continued to refuse to listen to his demands for independence.

The Amritsar massacre of 1919 was a warning of what could happen to anyone who challenged British authority. However, Gandhi refused to give up. He was now the most popular man in India. The Indian people trusted the "mahatma" to lead them. At public meetings and through his writings, Gandhi urged Indians to continue to stand up to the British using nonviolent means. In 1920, Gandhi was elected president of the Indian National Congress (INC), a political party that campaigned for independence. It adopted Gandhi's policy of nonviolent noncooperation.

QUICK FACTS

- Gandhi led protests designed to urge Great Britain to grant India its independence.
- He also campaigned for the rights of the Untouchables and of Indian Muslims.

FATHER OF THE PEOPLE

Gandhi traveled throughout India's 1.5 million square miles (3.8 million sq km). He preached his message of nonviolent noncooperation to everyone he met. He urged Indians not to buy British goods and to start spinning their own cloth. The British were furious about his message.

In 1922, Gandhi was sentenced to six years in jail for encouraging people to break the law. Gandhi continued to spin cotton in jail. In January 1924, he fell sick with appendicitis. Once he recovered, the British decided to release him in case he fell sick again. Gandhi went back to work.

A guard stands outside a prison where Gandhi was held.

Although Gandhi spent most of his time at home, Indians were always eager to hear his views on political events.

LONG-STANDING DIVISION

Gandhi turned his attention to a problem that had caused difficulties in India for centuries: the split between Hindus and Muslims. The two religious groups had lived alongside one another for hundreds of years in India. However, they had a history of turning to violence to sort out their different religious beliefs. Gandhi wanted Indians to unite and start accepting one another. In order to make both sides pay attention, he began a fast in September 1924, drinking only water. As he grew weaker, leaders from both religions agreed to put aside their differences and live peacefully together to save the health of the Mahatma.

THE SALT MARCH

The next turning point in Gandhi's campaign for independence came in 1930. On March 12, he set off from Ahmadabad to walk 240 miles (385 km) to Dandi on the Gujarat coast to collect salt from the beach. Gandhi wanted to draw attention to another unfair tax. In a hot country such as India, salt was vital to preserve food. The British not only placed a tax on salt but also made it illegal for people to collect salt found in salt pans around the coast. This forced Indians to pay the salt tax. Gandhi thought the tax unfair. He and his followers walked for a month to the coast. There, Gandhi picked up a handful of salt. Soon, thousands of people across India were collecting the naturally occurring salt.

Salt formed naturally in pans around the Indian coast.

After the Salt March, the British arrested up to 80,000 opponents of their taxes.

The British arrrested Gandhi. As **civil disobedience** spread across India, thousands of others were arrested, including Jawaharlal Nehru, who later became India's first prime minister. But the march was reported across the globe, and the arrests caused an outcry that proved Gandhi's influence in India to the British. *Time* magazine named Gandhi its man of 1930, and put his photograph on its cover.

Jawaharlal Nehru joined the Salt March.

QUIT INDIA

In 1931, Gandhi went to London for talks with the government to discuss independence for India. When he returned to India, the British authorities imprisoned him again. Gandhi criticized a British proposal to sideline the Untouchables by giving them their own political representatives. Gandhi was released when he started another fast.

In 1939, Britain declared war on Germany. This involved India in World War II (1939–1945). Gandhi asked why Britain was fighting for the freedom of other nations when it would not grant India its freedom. In 1942, Gandhi started the "Quit India" movement to pressurize the British into leaving.

Visiting northern England in 1931, Gandhi met workers at a cotton mill.

British soldiers fire at protestors from the Quit India movement.

Although Gandhi intended the movement to be nonviolent, violence against the British erupted across India. Gandhi was jailed once again, along with Kasturba. Kasturba got sick in jail and died on February 22, 1944. She had been married to Gandhi for more than 60 years.

FREEDOM

When World War II ended in 1945, Great Britain was broke. It could no longer afford to pay for its vast empire. The British prepared to grant India its independence. The biggest obstacle was the refusal of Muslims and Hindus to live together. The solution was to create a separate country for Muslims, called Pakistan. At midnight on August 15, 1947, India became independent. Meanwhile Pakistan became a new country.

The Partition OF INDIA

Tensions had existed between Muslims and Hindus in India since the 1200s, when Muslim rulers set up a kingdom in northern India.

Although Hindus remained in a majority in India, the country was also home to millions of Muslims. Despite their differences, the two groups had mostly lived together peacefully for centuries. In 1909, the British introduced "separate electorates." Muslims and Hindus elected their own representatives to separate government councils. This meant there was no united resistance to British rule. It also helped to increase the divide between the two religious groups.

Gandhi meets the Muslim leader Muhammad Ali Jinnah.

Millions of people gave up their homes and jobs to travel to either India or Pakistan.

As independence came closer, Gandhi argued that both groups could continue to live together in India. However, the leader of the Muslims, Muhammad Ali Jinnah, insisted that Indian Muslims should be given their own country, Pakistan. On its independence, India was split. The new country of Pakistan was carved out of Punjab in the west and Bengal in the east.

Fourteen million people were forced to relocate. Hindus and Sikhs in the north moved south to India, while Muslims in India moved north to Pakistan. Muslims and Hindus fought bitterly. Estimates suggest as many as 2 million people died during **Partition**. Millions more became homeless **refugees**.

Father of THE NATION

Gandhi believed that India's religious differences could be solved without dividing the country. His message cost him his life.

Gandhi had campaigned for Indian independence since his return from South Africa in 1914. When India finally became independent in August 1947, however, Gandhi refused to take part in the independence celebrations in the capital, Delhi. Instead, he spent Independence Day, August 15, in Calcutta (present-day Kolkata) in eastern India, fasting and praying. He was completely opposed to partition. While Gandhi had been supported by the majority of Indians in his fight for independence, however, he was almost alone in opposing the division of the country.

QUICK FACTS

- Gandhi's support for Muslims left in India made him unpopular with some Hindus.
- An **extremist** shot Gandhi dead in 1948.

VIOLENT DAYS

Following Independence Day, violence broke out across India and Pakistan as Hindus and Muslims fought one another. On August 31, a Hindu mob attacked the place Gandhi was staying in Calcutta. They were angry that he supported Muslims remaining in India. Gandhi decided that the only way to respond to the violence was to begin a long-term fast. As news spread through Calcutta, young people formed peace groups to end the violence. They asked Gandhi if he had a message for the rioters. He replied, “My life is my message.”

Riots broke out in many Indian cities following independence.

When Gandhi fasted, he ate and drank only the minimum needed to stay alive.

WORKING FOR PEACE

Within 72 hours, Gandhi's fast had helped restore peace to Calcutta. Rioting was still taking place in Delhi, so Gandhi went to the capital. He was shocked to find the city full of Hindu refugees who had fled from what was now Pakistan. He was horrified by the violence between Hindu and Muslim neighbors. Gandhi visited the injured in hospitals—both Hindus and Muslims—and listened to their stories.

ANOTHER FAST

As 1948 began, the violence had not ended. Gandhi once again decided to begin a fast. He declared that he would go without food until there was peace between India and Pakistan. On the sixth day of his fast more than 100 leaders from different political and religious groups visited Gandhi. They urged him to start eating again, and promised the violence would end. Gandhi was now 78 years old. The fast had clearly weakened him, and everyone was desperate to see him eat again.

Gandhi visits a Muslim shrine three days before his death.

On January 20, 1948, as Gandhi spoke at evening prayers, a bomb went off nearby. No one was hurt. The bomb had been planted by a Hindu extemist, Narayan Apte. Many extreme Hindus had turned against Gandhi because they were angry that he was so **tolerant** toward Muslims.

The Star — Late Night — Closing Prices

No 18,589 ** One Penny

GANDHI IS SHOT DEAD

THEY HEARD IN SILENCE

The news of Gandhi's death was announced at India House today and these Indians, gathered in the library, stood in silent tribute before a picture of the Mahatma. (See Star Man's Diary.)

Riots in Bombay after Hindu assassin fires at prayer meeting

GANDHI, India's apostle of non-violence, was assassinated in New Delhi today.

Gandhi's murder was headline news around the world.

ASSASSINATED

On January 30, 1948, Gandhi set out for evening prayers, supported by his grandnieces. A man approached and fired three bullets into Gandhi's chest. Gandhi fell to the ground and died, saying, "Hey Ram! (Oh God!)." India's prime minister, Jawaharlal Nehru, announced the news of Gandhi's death on the radio: "The light has gone out of our lives, and there is darkness everywhere.... Our beloved leader, Bapu as we called him, the father of the nation, is no more."

A line of footprints and a shrine mark the place where Gandhi died.

THE WORLD MOURNS

On February 2, 1948, more than 2 million people joined Gandhi's 5-mile (8 km) funeral procession. Following Hindu ritual, Gandhi's body was **cremated** on the bank of the Jumna River. Gandhi's ashes were then scattered at the meeting of the holy rivers Jumna and Ganges.

It was not just in India that news of Gandhi's **assassination** caused great sadness. The news made headlines across the world. The *New York Times* said: "What we can now say is that the enormous impact of Gandhi's personality on humanity, as the flood of tributes to him has shown, gives us the strong hope that the yearning for peace and goodwill still lives, still strives and will survive."

Gandhi's coffin was covered in the Indian flag.

The man who killed Gandhi was a Hindu **nationalist** named Nathuram Godse. He was tried for murder and found guilty. Gandhi's sons asked for Godse's life to be spared, but the judge ignored their request. Godse and Narayan Apte, who had carried out the bombing before the assassination, were both hanged in 1949.

Gandhi had only a few possessions when he died.

GANDHI'S LEGACY

Since his death, Gandhi's teachings have inspired world leaders such as Martin Luther King Jr. in the United States, Nelson Mandela in South Africa, and Aung San Suu Kyi in Burma. They all used nonviolent methods to achieve change. Gandhi also showed that it was necessary to make personal sacrifices. He spent nearly seven years in prison because of his beliefs. He owned fewer than 10 objects, including his watch, his sandals, and his walking stick, and he never owned his own house. Gandhi followed his own teaching about a life of simplicity. As he had said, "My life is my message."

Timeline

1869
- Born in Porbandar, Gujarat, on October 2.

1883
- Aged 13, Gandhi marries Kasturba.

1887
- Gandhi graduates from school but drops out of college.

1888
- Sails to England to study law.

1891
- Gandhi passes his law exams in London and returns to India.

1893
- Gandhi takes a one-year contract to work in South Africa.
- In May, Gandhi is thrown off a train in South Africa for traveling in first class.

1899
- The Boer War begins. Gandhi organizes an ambulance corps of Indian volunteers.

1906
- South Africa introduces the Black Act, which discriminates against Indians.

1913
- Gandhi organizes a successful strike of Indian coal miners in South Africa.

1914
- The Indian Relief Act undoes the provisions of the Black Act.

1915
- Gandhi moves back to India, where he receives a hero's welcome. He founds the Sabarmati Ashram.

1919
- Strikes break out in India against new British laws.
- On April 13, British troops shoot dead 379 Indian civilians and wound more than a 1,000 in what becomes known as the Amritsar Massacre.

1920	• Gandhi is elected president of the Indian National Congress.
1921	• Gandhi begins to wear the dhoti loincloth.
1922	• Gandhi is sentenced to six years in prison.
1924	• Gandhi is released after falling sick. • He fasts to achieve better relations between Hindus and Muslims.
1930	• Gandhi is arrested again after staging the Salt March against a British tax on salt.
1931	• Gandhi visits London to discuss independence.
1942	• Founds the Quit India movement.
1944	• Kasturba dies in prison.
1947	• India and Pakistan become independent at midnight on August 15. • When Gandhi criticizes Partition, a mob attacks the place where he is staying.
1948	• A bomb explodes close to where Gandhi is speaking. Ten days later, he is shot dead by a Hindu extremist. Two million people attend Gandhi's funeral.

KEY PUBLICATIONS

- *Indian Home Rule* (*Hind Swaraj*, 1909)
- *Indian Opinion* (journal, 1919-1931)
- *Young India* (journal, 1919-1932)
- *The Story of My Experiments with Truth* (two parts, 1927 and 1929)
- *The Collected Works of Mahatma Gandhi* (100 volumes, 1960-1994)

Glossary

activist Someone who campaigns to achieve political or social change.

ashram A religious retreat.

assassination A murder carried out for a political reason.

barrister A lawyer who is qualified to argue cases in court.

caste One of the classes of Hindu society in India, into which people were born and were unable to change.

civil disobedience A refusal to obey laws seen as being unfair.

colony A region or country governed by another country.

cremated Disposed of a dead body by burning it.

discrimination The unfair treatment of a group of people based on their race, religion, or other factors.

extremist A person who holds extreme views and may support the use of violence.

fasting Not eating or drinking.

independence A situation in which a country governs itself.

loincloth A male garment formed by a single piece of cloth wrapped around the hips.

loyalty A strong feeling of support for a country, individual, or cause.

massacre The violent killing of many people.

merchant Someone who earns a living from trade.

mobilized Gathered and organized a group of people for action.

mutiny A revolt by military personnel against their senior commanders.

nationalist Someone who supports political independence for a country.

outcast Someone who has been rejected by society.

Partition The division of India into India and Pakistan.

professional Belonging to an occupation with long training and a formal qualification.

refugees People who have been forced to leave their homes by violence, war, or persecution.

strike A refusal to work by employees as a protest against their employers.

tolerant Willing to allow the existence of other people's opinions or beliefs.

Further Resources

Books

Diemer, Lauren. *Gandhi*. New York: Av2 by Wiegl, 2014.

Doeden, Matt. *Darkness Everywhere: The Assassination of Mohandas Gandhi*. Minneapolis, MN: Twenty-First Century Books, 2007.

Green, Jen. *Gandhi and the Quit India Movement: Days of Decision*. Chicago: Capstone Heinemann Library, 2013.

Kuhn, Betsy. *The Force Born of Truth: Mohandas Gandhi and the Salt March*. Minneapolis, MN: Twenty-First Century Books, 2010.

Rau, Dana Meachen. *Who Was Gandhi?* New York: Grosset and Dunlap, 2014.

Websites

Ducksters
www.ducksters.com/biography/mohandas_gandhi.php
A biography of Gandhi's career for students.

History.com
www.history.com/topics/mahatma-gandhi
A biography of Gandhi with videos, galleries, and other links.

World History Project
worldhistoryproject.org/topics/mahatma-gandhi
A detailed timeline of Gandhi's life and activism in South Africa and India.

Mohandas K. Gandhi
www.mkgandhi.org/main.htm
An index page to a large collection of resources about Gandhi's life and work.

Publisher's note to educators and parents: Our editors have carefully reviewed these websites to ensure that they are suitable for students. Many websites change frequently, however, and we cannot guarantee that a site's future contents will continue to meet our high standards of quality and educational value. Be advised that students should be closely supervised whenever they access the Internet.

Index